Freedom

By

Sonja Britton

Freedom

Delicate treasures
growing at random;
immaculate pleasures
glowing in blossom;
what values and measures
the greatest kingdom
but children's adventures
in peace and freedom.

Written for the cover art

All Artwork in this publication is by the Author

Acknowledgement

My deepest gratitude goes to the Moriarty Historical Society. Especially Tina Cates-Ortega, Angela Cook, Elaine Ramsey, and Cyndi Waite for their encouragement, typing, editing, organizing, and performing as an agent for me.

I want to thank my friends online for their compliments, which helped me believe in my worthiness as a poet. Especially Joy Melendy, Jonathan Odermann for coaching and encouragement. Thank you to Joan Woodruff for her coaching and encouragement, also Ben and Sandi Steinlage for their assistance getting my book on Amazon.

Table of Contents

Advice to New Writers

To new writers, one and all, ten things are needed to heed this call. First-have a skin that's tough as nails. Second- never be afraid to fail. Third- have an endless love of words. Fourth- be aware of passive verbs. Fifth- or a quart, for loosening writer's block. For nothing helps when you watch the clock. Sixth- commas, you'll never get them right. Seventh- just write for your own delight. Eighth- if you don't like it, they won't either. Ninth- it's a talent; no, you don't have a fever. Tenth - just so you'll know it, if you think you're a poet and you try to rhyme everything. Make sure your words say what you mean!

My Words

My words are simple because that's who I am. They are not complicated or abstract, except when I go off the deep end. I know there is nothing new under the sun, it's all been said or done before.

However, if my words touch a heart, mend a pain, state a feeling that many have felt, and a person relates, feels a connection with what I say, if it soothes them, embraces them...and they know that I know how they feel. My words have served their purpose...simple as they are.

Simply Put

What I have to say
is nothing new
It's been said before
I know that's true.

But for the simple man
verses written in riddle
are hard to understand
and tell us very little.

We are the simple folks
with "Hard Knocks" degrees.
We laugh hard at our jokes,
eat cornbread and black-eyed peas,
and authors blessed in their forte
need not take up our time,
trying to decipher word charades
they have played with rhyme.

For you and I know
what matters in life
is love to grow
'tween husband and wife
a girl, a boy, to carry on genes.

Friends to share joy
that good times bring.
To help when in need
and comfort in pain
some rain and sunshine
a home to contain.

Some gain, some failure
and as important
as all the above
is to give your neighbor
respect and love.

And with God's blessings
good health to remain
We'll leave this world better
than when we came.

Where Do I Begin?

As colors of rain
so beautifully bend
I run in circles
chasing the ends.

Painting my message
writing with pen.
Such running over,
where do I begin?

Art

Art flows from the soul
gives dreams substance
visual reality of what is not.
Art saves the moment
the conception forever.

Blue wolves or black blossoms
or tears falling up,
Whatever the dreamer dreams
evolves from nothing
to be...forever.

No matter who the artist
or how great,
The visions of the soul
are free to this world
will be...forever.

A viewer may know
the dream of the dreamer,
or be lost in the myth,
Searching for the message
from the soul
Perhaps...forever.

I Must

I am charged with writing these words.
I have no real choice.
They come to me in the night.
They disturb my sleep.
I'm asked to portray life in color;
detailed in black and white.
I could lie and speak only of beauty,
but the truth is sometimes gray.
I am compelled by truth.

It's my duty to tell it like it is!
To perhaps undress a woman,
covered by clothing for middle age.
expose her sagging breast and
child-stretched stomach to the world,
without demeaning her with my words.

I argue with ugliness, the cause of regret.
I don't want to describe it!
However; truth is sometimes ugly!
I am burdened with revealing truth
exciting, mundane, repulsive, flaunted
or concealed...in your face truth!

Perhaps...strip the peacock of his pride,
serve him plucked, breaded and deep fried!
To describe beauty and joy
with insufficient words that can't.
To raze the structure of denial
flattened to the level of truth.

I am charged to be the conscience,
the mentor, the lover, the soul.
I must turn over the secret stones,
Thrust my fingers into black soil
hidden beneath for years;
and broadcast Mother Earth
undressed, fertile and ready.

I am charged with probity,
with describing the unseen,
with revealing the face behind the mask.
I'm to expose the truth behind excuse,
find the real reason for fear and hate
And in the end...perhaps revealing mine.

Sharing

If I can put in words today
a message you need to hear.
If I can find just what to say
to ease your pain and fear,
then all the years of searching
the gray matter I possess,
and in defeat at last researching
the books upon my desk.
I will feel and share the joy
writers before me have felt
when you grasp the thought I employ
and share the gift I'm dealt.

Cold Tech

This is a new experience for me.
Now my words are
remote
mechanical
no longer extended
from my soul
formed of
my character
separate
sterile
cold
must warm them
from the outside
not easy
takes talent
color
mixing
brush stokes
bold
no blue
allowed.

Just God's World
and Me...

Oh to linger there,
to breathe deeply
the mountain air.
To leave all else behind
and not be burdened
with the daily grind.
To close my eyes and listen
to nature's melody.
Then to gaze, eyes full of glisten
at a sky unspoiled by man.

"Mmmm Good"

Morning mountain mist
manipulating my mind.
Magic moments moving
memories through time.
Moist air mothering
life sublime.
Master the merit
of each moment.
Mine.

Miracle

Lord, how do we thank you?
We should be on our knees!
But as I watched raindrops puddled
I prayed for, if You please.

The grass will soon show green.
Dessert flowers stretch to bloom,
and ranchers will do a dance.
Their cattle will fatten soon.

Corn will rise in straight rows,
alfalfa will sway in the wind.
Your miracle of monsoon
is life giving once again.

Only us dessert dwellers
know the treasure you have sent.
We've watched the sky and prayed.
The scent of rain our sins repent.

Since I'm called an "old timer".
It was faith…I knew You'd act.
I've seen it many times before.
I knew rain would come…that's a fact.

Watch carefully for it comes fast,
the miracle of monsoon.
The dessert will grow surprises.
Attention now…they'll come soon.

Dear Lord, we come to thank You
for this blessing You have sent.
In Jesus name we pray,
it keeps coming 'till it's spent.

Amen

First Nature

Man dreams of peace while he loads his gun.
The bear dreams of many streams in which the salmon run.
The salmon dreams of just one thing - to finish what was begun,
for it's the nature of the beast
within the cycle of the sun,
that hunger lingers in search of feast
and mortality makes us one.

Raven

A raven has landed in my tree!
He's black, black as black can be!
His yellow eyes glaring down at me!
His raspy voice declaring, scolding me!
He sharpens his beak upon my branches.
He gives to me discomforting glances.
And flies away proclaiming he's free!

My Valley

Cotton candy clouds,
mountains in cobalt shrouds,
alizarin blossoms top cacti
while the scent of pine floats by.

Sassy mountain jays
run other birds away,
and my heart smiles
as I watch my valley play.

The morning breeze
caressing trees,
will turn to wind soon,
and later in the afternoon
may even bring monsoon.

The sweet smell of mountain air
washed clean when it rained,
precious moisture everywhere,
my valley again sustained.

A Late Walk

Long shadows of evening
caress new emerald grasses.
Fence posts run together
as another day passes.
I hear sounds of life
swiftly rushing by me.
Wonder what the future
will offer or deny me?

A lovely stand of mallow
waves gently in the breezes,
and a cocky old crow
rides the wind as he pleases.
The sun is sewing golden lace
'round a dark blue evening cloud
as I walk here in this beauty,
say my thoughts again…out loud.

Now I can smell the rain
as it falls upon my neighbor.
No more thoughts about tomorrow,
it's this day that I must savor.

Opals in the Sky

In the last light
of a day gone by
just to welcome night
and to say goodbye
were colors refracting
from clouds so high
'twas the eves enacting
of an Opal Sky.

A Day's End

Sunlight kissing the world goodnight
causing it to blush.
Shadow playing with the light
in the evening hush.
Crickets setting rhythm
for the dancing of the stars.
And voices of the night
sing the notes upon the bars.

County Fair

Three foot cowboys in ten gallon hats
wear long legged jeans and western boots,
straddle their horses with bellies fat,
and wait on edge for calves in chutes.

Miniature farmers in striped overalls
are washing and grooming three hundred pound hogs.
Country kids, cleaning their stalls
anxiously wait on auctioneer calls.

Ladies scurrying with arms full of flowers
some artfully arranged, brought for judging.
Plates full of goodies all made of flour
carried by daughters with mothers nudging.

Pickles and beets, beans and jellies,
Afghans, doilies, quilts and vases,
lovingly made to tempt the bellies,
and all displayed to delight faces.

Cucumbers, onions, squash and potatoes,
in every shape, color, and size,
pumpkins, melons, beets and tomatoes,
planted and watered and fertilized.

Artists hoping the world will discover,
displaying their souls within their crafts
Tables set up under tents to cover
serve hot dogs and burgers in afternoon drafts.

Blue ribbons and trophies at last awarded
bring squeals of delight and bright shiny eyes!
All the hard work and effort rewarded
when the County Fair gives them a prize!

A Remnant of Heritage

His eyes have a fixed squint,
from years of New Mexico sun,
yet sparkle like a struck flint,
with down-home sense and pure fun.

He's not counterfeit; he's the real "McCoy",
not Marshal Dillon or John Wayne,
but a pure-blooded, genuine, real cowboy.
Truly the one who deserves the fame!

He's tough, had to be, but caring.
Now he talks to me about good ol' times –
ropin, brandin', a "green" horse rarin' –
tears cloud the sparkle; roll down weathered lines.

He swallows hard – stiffens in his chair,
And I…searching his priceless rugged face,
feel his pain, as we're sitting there,
and I wonder, who will take his place?

Who'll ride out and look for strays,
or rise before dawn to check mother cows?
Who'll "heel" calves on brandin' days,
or haul hay on Christmas behind snow plows?

And who will the little boys look up to?
Who'll tell them how it used to be?
Who'll set an example that won't undo,
and preserve the heritage he's given me?

I wonder…as I set here with him,
listening to time roaring past history,
I wonder…
Will the future remember him?

In Memory of Burrel Chaney

17

Estancia Valley

Maybe she's not so grand as some
but to those of us who love her,
she's second place to none.

They named her Estancia Valley
and that ain't easy to understand.
They must 'a had a beer in their bellies
and eyes plumb full of sand,
'cause a rancher here pinches every penny
n' counts ever blade 'a grass,
n' prays to God above that
what he's got'll last.

N' when he's ready for market
it's likely the bottoms out.
N' he knows for sure he can't make it through
the winter or summer's drought.

N' if you think that's bad you ain't heard nothin' yet.
The farmer in this valley never knows what he'll get,
but he plants his crop, and prays that a late freeze don't get it.
He waters, n' weeds, n' sprays so the hoppers don't eat it.

Dawn to dark make up his days
n' when harvest times upon it.
Monsoon rains move in to stay
n' there ain't no way to cut it.
Nobody 'round wants mildewed hay
n' he'd just as well forget it.

N'them Colorado winters ain't got nothn' over us.
Kids goin' to school need a four-wheel drive bus.
N' spring ain't sprung 'fore summers begun
n' summer is dry n' baked hard by the sun.

Horned toads, locoweed, n' rattlesnakes
n' blown' ya over winds, choilla,
prickly pear, n' yucca
will show ya' they're not friends.

You'd better have what it takes
if you've come here to stay.
To "make it" in this place friend,
it's the only way.

Now, I've been here since '44
and I often wonder why,
one reason is the people
another is the sky.

Bigger hearts can't be found nor better friends
when you luck is down. They're proud n' strong and gentle,
n' lovin', n' warm as bread fresh from the oven.
N' when you sit and talk 'bout happenin's of the day
they listen with their eyes and mean what they say.

N' when you go to visit you'll find an open door.
Just as you're 'about to leave
they'll ask you to stay some more.

N' if you get sick
n'think you're surely gonna die
there'll be some of those friends
a standin' right close by.

Folks that love, n' folks that are kind,
n' folks that care when you cry.
Folks like that are hard to find
in a world that lives on lies.

N' you know, that song called
America 'bout Purple Mountain Majesty
bet it was written right here 'cause that's shore what I can see,
those big ole' Rocky Mountains so perty over there.

I watch em' every mornin' from my favorite rockin' chair.
N' floatin in the sky colored pink by mornin' sun
are the biggest fluffy clouds ever seen by anyone.

N' the sweetest mountain air lingers on from the night
n' floats through my winda' as I watch them clouds turn white.

N' the sky turns the deepest blue like a water hole I once seen.
N' it spreads all over tarnation to the end of the earth it seems.
N' the sunsets well, they're the kind
no dang artist can paint as fine.

Only GOD can swing a brush like that
color you'll never forget. Flame red, violet,
pink, n' blue, orange, n' peach, n' yella too
rise up from behind the "Rockies" turn the deepest purple hue.

God, I love it! He knows I do.
N' I think of the history this valley has seen.
Why, I sit where the ancients n' dinosaurs have been.
N' Spanish explorers searchin' treasure here in,
n' wagon trains of homesteaders surrounded by Indians.

N' "Route 66" brought Model A Fords right through here "way
back when." Now I-40 sports Cadillacs n' 18 wheelers goin' east,
n' west, n' end to end.

N' I'm lookin' at the sky that our Apollo's flown in.
Well, folks, that's shore enough to make one really proud.
N' although times can be tough, I'll stand before any crowd.
I won't hesitate to tally; I'll shout it right out loud.
I'm proud of Estancia Valley and the people it's endowed.

Sideline Poet

When is a poet a cowboy or cowboy a poet?
Wonder which comes first as I question yet again?
It is difficult I ponder, the answer I don't know it.
Does talent emerge with a cow and a pen?

Is one born a poet and then a rancher he becomes
or is the rancher born with talent to spare?
To qualify for both cowboy and poet in one's name,
must one have gifts of rhyme and have cows to care?

To qualify for both cowboy and poet in one's name,
must one be hands-on or just repeating?
May a wanna be like me write their stories the same
or is my effort possibly defeating.

I was a young thing in a tiny apron and a white uniform
when I began to love cowboys, hats an' boots.
From the sideline just listenin' an opinion began to form,
and I dearly wanted to be in cahoots!

I longed from the sidelines, and I even once raised a cow,
and I served a lot of steaks to boys that wore a hat.
I listened to their stories, and thought, "Could I be somehow?"
I wished so much that I could share some of that.

Nothing fake among them, was no pretense about those men.
They were what they were, didn't care what was thought.
When they came in for coffee I knew where they had been.
They smelled of cow and sweat, which cannot be bought.

One day they had pulled a calf, the cow couldn't do it alone.
They were proud the baby would live another day,
their heifer would still be there to help pay that bank loan.
T'was tales of profit told not poetry that day.

21

Most of those men were cowboys, but poets they were not,
at Sunday dinner as I listened to them talk.
I dreamed and wished someday I'd join them and have my spot.
From just listening, maybe I could walk the walk.

Well I did get a horse and learned to ride maybe just enough,
watched my kid's rodeos, and horse shows and I was proud.
Those cowboys helped them to cowboy up; they became tough.
I'm still on the sidelines sometimes dreaming out loud.

But in my heart still lives their stories, I treasure every word.
Still want to be one as I recall their words today.
None rhymed or metered yet it was poetry that I heard.
When I tell their stories I tell them my way.

No answers to that question here, I hope you find your own
for I humbly stand on the sideline still looking in.
Now I'm too old to find my spot and that for sure is known.
Cowboy, if you're a poet write it so it won't end.

A Lost Treasure

Grasses of delicate chain in hues of "Black Hills" gold,
dance like cobras, trained, doing exactly what they're told.
Swaying in the wind, standing tall on end,
and clustered in their mist gathering the last sun,
are asters carved in "Amethyst" standing proud for anyone.

Even the lowly tumbleweed,
in preparation to spread its seed,
appears to be transplanted from sea.
Its branches of "Coral" in shades of reds,
reaching above, waving golden heads.

Along my path, as far as I can see,
are golden sunflowers, tall as me.
Bravely facing what they know will be,
and at their feet lie brassy leaves, tarnished rusty reds,
with touches of "Jade" not wanting to leave,
clinging to their beds.

On my way back, cordially waving goodbye,
are "Platinum" fingers of Winter Fat
sparkling like diamonds, reflecting the sky,
letting everyone know right where they're at.

Wherever I look, lost treasure abound
as I span my valley, there all around
are "Lapis" mountains that form its bounds.
They're sporting new color within the blue.
Golden matrix is laced, through and through.

More lovely treasure calling so bold,
and who can resist the calling of "Gold."
Cedar, fir, and pine, of "Emerald" so green,
standing tall, all along the highway.
Golden cottonwoods, are easily seen
in the canyon, as I go my way,
and pushy chamisa, crowding for space,
is of tarnished silver, tipped in "Gold" lace.

Getting closer and closer, on I climb,
toward the treasure I hope to find.
Before me, the roadside trees
are wearing "Rubies" if you please,
carved and strung like "vining" leaves,
and draped so casually for all to see.

And proud Sumac, not to be out done,
is flaunting its "Garnet" leaves
and "Coral" seed pods in the sun.
Blue spruce stand, so exquisitely dressed,
in nothing but their very best,
each needle carved of a "Turquoise" sliver.
Such beauty, surely, will last forever.

All at once, I can't help but stare,
gold, pure gold, is everywhere!
Aspens, with beautiful trunks of "ivory"
dangling their treasure right beside me!
"Gold Leaf" treasure, all around me!
And I'm as "rich" as anyone could be.

Now you must know of the treasures I speak,
lost one year ago, found this week.
Here in New Mexico, in autumn, to seek.

Indian Summer Joy

It was Indian summer joy
freedom granted a little boy
to walk among the asters bloom
and encroach upon the turtle's room.

So precious are the little things
that only freedom brings
so fleeting is the moment's joy
and fragile is the bloom.

Drummer

Spirits of Peace

Those who've walked this way before
in spirit are touching my heart.
They call to me to search for more
then take me to a world apart.

They live within the sand and rock
and have sisters in the sky,
and whisper now in spirit talk
of time and years gone by.

They walk with me among the thorns
to touch silk blossoms there,
and beckon me to what adorns
far mountains that look bare.

I cannot hear the noise of greed
nor feel the fear of death.
When spirits call I feel no need
but linger there short of breath.

The spirits of peace dwelling here
watch over this beautiful land
and cast a spell on those who dare
encounter their magic hand.

Spirits of Enchantment

Ancient ghosts haunt these canyons
while ships of space fly overhead,
and cities grow to house the millions
upon the graves where lie the dead.

Above valleys stretching to infinity
are ancient mesa dwellings,
and if we listen carefully,
we'll hear voices so compelling.

Spirits of rock and adobe walls
live in the dust that's lying,
and on and on their history calls
from in the wind that's flying.

Past centuries they've rested here,
their voices carry in the wind,
and if we listen close we'll hear
enchanting messages they send.

Messages from the mountain's peak,
over deserts to rivers grand,
their voices luring us to seek
the magic of this land.

Sidewinder

I had mare named Sidewinder and you can imagine why we named
her that.
I swear that mare could jump 8 feet sideways over a stinkin' little
rat.
She would also apply her brakes in the darnedest places, over
nothin at all!
When she's done we're starein' eye to eye and there was nothin' to
break my fall.

One time while ridin'; relaxed with her rhythm, things were
so...peaceful
she spots a rattler, n' sideways we go; I'm ridin' air, grabbin' mane
by the handful!
When she finally hits ground she's runnin' full out; headin' for
Lobo hill!
I'm still on board; don't know how, "whoa!" didn't work and I'm
feelin' the urge to kill.

The rest of the crew were tryin' to catch her but it's hard to ride
laughin' out loud.
It was quite a sight me scared spit-less and them laughin' through a
dust cloud.
"Winder" finally wound down and I thought she might just
founder.
I'm red faced angry with hysterical cowboys all standin' around
her!

Sidewinder was a mustang mare and in the end she suited me.
No blue blood runs through my veins either that anyone can see.
She was independent, full of surprises, and very head strong.
I'm just like her, my hubby surmises, that's why we got along.

A Man Such As He

He knows me
and at the sound of my voice
he acknowledges me.

A man such as he thinks I'm worthy
of a place in his mind.
This man who walks in darkness
because he is blind.

This man who fought for me
in a foreign war,
came back without his sight
but never really lost his way
because he never lost the light.
A man such as he
acknowledges me.

This man who chose to ranch
for his living,
Who has lived his life
by sharing and giving.
This man who can climb
his windmill by braille
can find every rung
and count every nail.
A man such as he
acknowledges me.

This man who mounts his horse
to parade old glory
to a rallying crowd that
doesn't know his story.
This man who has never known
he had limits.

He who has climbed every climb,
and reached all the summits.
A man such as he
acknowledges me.

So undeservingly,
I will stand proud
when he sets me apart
From the rest in the crowd.
for I know there is also a place in his heart
that he has graciously given to me.
A man such as he
acknowledges me.

Written for Louis O'Neal

The Mayor Was a Cowboy

In a high desert valley
with blue mountains all around,
a village grew made up of two.
its citizens desired one town.

Moriarty became incorporated,
  all together with one name.
A government was then needed
so cowboys, farmers and others came.

They signed up to rule our city,
  then our first election took place.
Brave men ran for Mayor and Council,
  it really wasn't much of a race.

But I think what spoke of our culture,
  was the man who held the gavel
wore a Stetson, chaps and spurs
on his boots and had a horse to travel.

Yep… our first Mayor was a cowboy
  A little rough around the edges.
He sat at the head…gavel in hand.
Decisions were made with no hedges.

He ruled like he handled his rope,
if someone strayed he pulled 'em in.
Moriarty grew and prospered too
  And we watched it all begin.

In memory of Lawrence Groff

The Mayor Was a Cowboy

Coffee Time in Cowboy Country

It's coffee time once again, they saunter in one by one. The waitress knows their names, which one takes cream…which one none. They gather at their table, proudly lean back in their chairs. It's coffee time in cowboy country, and they're here to get their share.

First one hails from Texas, which leaves him often braggin';
but cowboys at this table all suffer from tongue waggin'.

This one's big and proud, his hair has a sliver sheen.
 He sits tall in his chair, pretends to be tough and mean;
but his heart is made of gold, and melts at the touch of a child.
 A grandpa now ten times, brags of sowin' oats young and wild.

He still has some horses, and rides 'em now and then.
He still likes to talk of ropin' and will betcha he can win;
but they ain't about to take him on, for fear what he says it true.
They remember how once he was, and the respect he has is due.

Now at mornin' coffee he sits here with his old cronies,
talks about the good ol' days and who had the best ponies.
He still swears that it was his, yet knows they don't believe him.
Each cowboy's horse is best, that he'll just have to give them.

The next one's small in stature that tells nothing of his worth.
He was raised a cowboy in the roughest country on earth.
He's the best horse trader on this side o' the Rio Grande;
perhaps the other side too, maybe the whole dad-blamed land.

There ain't many cowboys that can beat him in a deal,
'cause he knows all about horses, and how to give a good spiel;
and he can read people 'bout as good as he can a horse,
knows when to reign 'em in, when to keep 'em on course.

Such talents make good stories, and a teller he's become.
He loves to tell a joke and is the first to laugh at some.
Even if the joke falls flat, soon laughter spreads the table,
his laugh is so contagious, and to resist it they're unable.

Just across sits an Okie, and they won't let him forget,
he's worse n'any Texan, when it comes to strechin' it.
He has no horses now, and he must rely on the past,
and when he starts relyin', they wonder how long it'll last.
Now, as his story goes, his horse coulda beat 'em all,
and to hear him tell it, must've been twenty hands tall.
Was faster than lightin', not just leavin' that ol' box,
goes this Okie's story, of how he'd fill up his socks.
Yep, his loop goes a flyin' just as far as he does dare,
and the Okie keeps on braggin', and the drinkers just don't care.

They know where he came from, and they know he came late.
 He ain't impressin' no one, they watched him from the gate.
They know what filled his socks wasn't money but his fear,
so they let him have his day, over coffee with them here.

The waitress stops by now and then to check their coffee levels,
and the cowboys seize the moment to harass and give the devil.
The gal is a wise one though, and full of spunk and fun,
she comes back with a quip or two, and leaves laughin' on the run.

The fourth one is kinda quiet, he just snickers now and then.
He doesn't ride a horse, but races cars around a bend.
His ancestors rode 'em though, there's Indian in his veins.
They rode all around here, and on the Oklahoma plains.

He listens to the cowboy stories, seems to love 'em all.
I wonder if he ever wished his car was twenty-hands tall.
Perhaps war paint 'round the headlights,
his face painted like a chief,
his headdress swept back by the wind,
is that really beyond belief? No sir, not around this table.

They'd all listen very polite then they'd invite him out for a race
next Saturday night.

Now, chairs sit empty at their table today,
no more need for coffee, no more to say.
Stories are still told, of when they were here,
the cowboys still brag of friends they held dear.
But there'll be no more like those gone before,
or those telling the stories that we all adore.

In memory of Monroe Parker, Carl Cannon, Jerry Britton, and Thomas
Jr. Plant

There's a Pasture in Heaven

There's a pasture in Heaven
That is emerald green,
Where he rides now
No barbed wire is seen.

The wind won't be blowing
Gritty sand in his eyes.
As he sits in his saddle
And surveys heaven's skies.

We will miss him here
That's a truth unspoken.
He's touched many hearts
And has left many broken.

With God as his foreman
He works his domain,
Sitting tall in the saddle
Riding free of pain.

Tribute to local cowboy Monroe Parker

For God's Soldier, Our Hero
"Pete" Pressly

I wish I had hugged him last Sunday
Like I had so many times before.
I wish I had told him I loved him
Before I walked on through the door.

I just shook his hand and said"Good Morning."
Unaware he'd not be there next week.
The Lord gives us no warning or
I would have kissed him gently on the cheek.

No, we had no way of knowing
His remaining days were so few,
And his mission here was over,
Finished, all through.

His life was an example to us all,
Spent in service and giving.
He made good use of God's allotment,
Taught us sharing is living.

He gave us laughter without ridicule
And comfort in our pain.
He gave us direction and serenity
In a world that is most insane.

He taught us with an open mind
And an open heart.
He made us search and question
Seek answers from the start.

He was a champion of God's word.
He was a soldier for the Lord.
He fought his battles with courage
Had no need for a sword.

He believed that our children
Were given with God's trust,
That we would love them and teach
Them that God's way is just.

He was a constant in a world
Racked with insecurity.
He was a young heart
Trapped in a body of maturity.

He was our hero, our mentor
And always, our friend.
The Lord has called him home
He was prepared, ready for the end.

Now, it is our job to honor him,
Live our lives as he showed us how.
The challenge will be tremendous.
The time to start is… now.

But I wish I had hugged him last Sunday
Like I had so many times before.
I wish I had told him I loved him
Before I walked on through the door.

Note: One time, after I had finished
reading a poem I had written to Pete
He said to me,
"You should write love songs."
*This is my **Love** song to him.*

Lady in Lace

She sits there so solemn
the lady in lace,
filled with mystique
adorned in grace.

I wonder what brings her
to this place,
and what secrets lie
behind the face.

She sits all alone
caught in her pose,
her fingers caressing
a single rose.

It's as if she is lost
in a secret repose,
and where she has ventured
No one knows.

Dressed as a bride
the lady in lace,
clings to her pride
perhaps in disgrace.

What loves lie hidden
and never embraced,
and what passions forbidden
the lady in lace.

Note: This was written about a model in art class. When I read it to our instructor he told me her story. She was a nun, she fell in love and left her promise to the Lord. Then her love left her. I felt this poem as I was painting her.

The Black Poet

There you were hiding
behind closed minds
from judgement
not abiding
unchanged by times.

Kept in your 'place'
by prejudice and fear.
Pains of your race
reflected in your tears.

So bright a mind
in a body abused.
A world too unkind
only goodness you used.

Conquered with a pen
and the magic of word
all of man's sin
while the whole
world heard.

In Tribute to Maya Angelou

Control

The big flat screen just sits there,
reflecting the windows behind.
my imagination plays as I stare.
It can tell me no lies as if I'm blind.

It manipulates, controls our minds.
We let it corrupt, poison our spirit.
Like sheep, we follow in lines,
no control of direction, they steer it.

It spews propaganda like it's a gift.
We anxiously open our surprise.
in our ignorance it causes a rift.
It fractures our country, families likewise.

We confuse reality with their slant
in the news, programs, and movies.
Brainwashing is presented in the rant,
they create mayhem with such ease.

We're inundated with their selection,
hundreds of channels we want or not.
Porn to infidelity is the projection.
We're told to take it all or we get squat.

It would be no more if I had my way.
What then could we do to fill our time?
Maybe we would find something to say.
I could paint, draw, write and rhyme!

Fate's Lady

Humped shouldered,
eyes searching the ground.
The bag lady stumbling
goes on her round.

But for a twist of fate
there goes a lady of grace,
dripping in furs and diamonds,
wearing satin and lace.

Her hand's in the bend
of a fine gentleman's arm,
poised with self-assurance,
and safe from all harm.

But now here she is,
dirty and rag-tagged,
going through trash,
worse than the dog dragged.

Her bed is made of concrete,
no linen and feathers.
She gives in to sleep
with one eye on the others.

No pillows or blankets,
just cold winds of night,
wrap round her body
curled up so tight.

And if she does wake
with the light of dawn,
she begins all over,
her search must go on.

In Sharing

I've laid bare my soul for you

and where is my soul today?

Is it safely hidden from view

or in a window on display?

All my secrets you must know,

all my fears, I told you so.

Are those secrets still intact?

Are my fears, now true, in fact?

And in these things which matter not,

all of us have shared.

What matters most to me

Is...have you ever cared?

So Little

It will mean so little, my passing,
no tracks will I leave behind.
Like the sand in which they're pressing,
with the wind there's none to find.
For eons to come in millions of years
when others will pass this way,
they'll not know that I've been here,
but by chance, they read what I say.

Heaven's Like…

I've often wondered…why gold streets
when there's no longer a demand.
I know Heaven has expectations to meet
but it's better to ride a horse on sand.
I like to believe that God's heaven will be
pleasing to each woman and man.
What is beauty to them, they will see
and be blessed by God's great hand.

The Plan

Such evidence of God's great plan…
Of life…death…life again,
in the peaceful passing of an autumn day's end,
in the promise of spring… new life to begin.

Jealousy

Jealousy is a monster

filled with rage,

bound by his fears

in a bar-less cage,

huddled in a corner

all ready to spring,

his helpless victim

such torment he'll bring.

Plummeting Metaphors

We're crowded into cities
yet lonelier than before.
Crowded into cities
with people door to door.
We're molded into patterns
so designed a metaphor.
Molded into to patterns
by patterns made before.
We plummet like pinballs
bumpered through our course.
Plummet like pinballs
recycled with remorse.

Plain and Simple

Fancy language

I may not understand,

Pompous pretension

that sounds so grand,

but the plight

of you and me

I understand quite well.

Of joy and sorrow

and pain I see,

and dreams of Heaven and Hell.

For thirst of love

and powers that be,

our souls we're willing to sell

while the Heaven we seek

lies under our nose,

and Hell is in the fears that dwell.

Butterfly

Ballerina of the sky
as you perform for me
I hear the music floating by
a lovely symphony.

Winged like an angel
in brilliant velvet hue
flowers form your stage
against a sky
of aqua blue.

No earth bound ballerina
could ever dance like you
or be so light
upon her feet
when her pirouette is due.

Ballerina of the sky
as I watch you dance today
I think how lucky
it was I
you chose to watch your play.

Politics

Shhhhhhh   it

Do da
Doda
Do da
Do

Do dung
Dodung
Do dung
Dung

Dung heap
Dungheap
Dung heap
Bull

Bull dung
Bulldung
Bull dung
Bull

Shhhhhhhh   it!

Desire

We search for you in all known places,

in all the hearts and all the faces,

in bouquets of flowers, glasses of wine,

in jewels of diamonds and pearls so fine.

We search for you in elegant graces,

in back alley bars, cold dark places,

in people unknown, strangers we find,

in failure we lastly search our own mind.

Temptation 1

Temptation is such a sneak!

Just when I think I've got it licked

and satisfaction has reached its peak,

there it stands all polished and slicked

and it makes my knees go weak!

Temptation 2

I CANNOT, I MUST NOT SUBMIT TO WHAT I FEEL!

If I do…pain will ensue and sorrow if I yield!

And all will know that I've done so, surely they can tell.

Temptation won what it has begun, and I have gone to hell.

Christmas Things

This year when it comes time
to pack Christmas "things" away,
and save the glitter and shine
for another Christmas Day,
please do not pack away,
all the love and the caring.

Don't pack away the warmth,
the giving, and the sharing.
Don't pack away compassion,
with the tinsel and the glitter,
although apathy's in fashion,
it gives no shelter in the winter.

Don't pack away your helping hand,
you may need it through the year,
to help out a starving man,
or someone you hold dear.

So wrap all your pretty "Christmas Things",
pack them carefully away,
but keep out all the "Important Things"
to use for every day.

Simple

It is so simple.
Why do we complicate it so?
We're to believe as a child believes.
God loves us.
God gave his son for us.
God offers us grace.
If we just believe.

Yet, we analyze, scrutinize, prioritize,
And categorize God's word to fit in
to our world,
to our way,
to our whim.

Interpretation is such a big word
and a bigger responsibility.
I pray for the Lord's grace
when I get it wrong.

God help us to understand
the simplicity of your love,
your boundless grace and forgiveness.
Give us tolerance, Lord,
that we may not be judgmental
of those who do not see your word our way.

For it really is so simple.
You're the only one
who has all the answers.

The Truth

My ego be damned

as it stands there so full of false pride!

Masked and programmed

so afraid to bare

the fears that live inside!

My ego and I both lied!

Apple Pie

I long for a nickel cup of coffee
and apple pie at fifteen cents a slice,
a Ship n' Shore blouse at two ninety-eight,
and a Poodle skirt on sale at half price.

I long for a time
when youth and innocence were synonymous
and children were expected to be nice;
when women wanted to be glamorous,
and teachers were respected not iced.

I long for a time
when virtue was a reality
and never a sacrifice;
when honesty was politically correct,
when integrity had no price.

I long for a time
when a man's word was prized more
than his possessions;
when we were proud to look each other in the eye,
when there was little room for concessions.

I long for a time
when 'America the Beautiful'
caused goosebumps, not riots;
when the 'Star Spangled Banner'
flew proudly from a pole
never covering the butt
of some lost drugged soul.

I long for a time
when to be an American
meant to be responsible;
no excuse, no way out.
Responsible for decisions, actions,
family, someone to depend on
with no doubt.

I long for a time
when right was right, wrong was wrong,
and there were no exceptions;
when the world was simply…simple,
and so few real deceptions.

I long for a time
when the boys chased the girls,
when being called someone's "Lady"
was truly an honor;
when 'turf' was a term for grass,
and grass was for picnics,
not the blood of some poor goner.

I long for a time
when hardships built character not prisons;
when we strived to overcome, not submit;
when we pulled together,
prayed together, and shared visions;
when challenge was a battle,
and courage conquered it.

I long for another time, another world,
a world to believe in, that I saved for me,
a world an innocent young girl
perhaps couldn't really see.

I long for a nickel cup of coffee
and apple pie at fifteen cents a slice,
a Ship n' Shore blouse at two ninety-eight;
and a 'Poodle' skirt would be real nice.

Foot Prints

Foot prints of my past
lie in the paths I take.
Have I learned at last?
when to follow, or to brake?
Do lessons of the past?
guide each step I make?
Can I, this day, grasp
each lesson for my sake?

Mystic Memories

Another time...another place
I know...I've been a princess once.
Once I had a different face,
rare jewels hung around my neck.

For I love the touch of silk
with the denim that I wear.
and I know beyond a doubt
I once had golden hair.

I withdraw from mystic memory
and as I navigate my trip,
I force my soul inhabitant
to bite her lower lip.

Another time...another place
she'll be back I know.
She must suffer my mistakes;
she must...in order to grow.

Thistles Grow

Thistles Grow

Thistles grow where little boys go
in search of treasures unknown.
They fill their pockets with rocks
for sky rockets
and pick blossoms from seeds not sown.
Yes, thistles grow where little boys go
but they leave the thistles alone.

Written for artwork "Thistles"

I Think of a Life Time

As I bathe in the sun
of the deep blue sky
and feel the coolness
of a cloud passing by,
I think of a lifetime
(thus emitting a sigh)
as I bathe in the sun
of the deep blue sky.

I think of a beautiful
little boy and girl,
and how in this realm
their lives have unfurled,
and I feel the coolness
of a cloud passing by,
and I think of a lifetime
(thus emitting a sigh).

I think of the past,
what's too late to change
I think of the future
what's left to arrange
And I think of a lifetime
(thus emitting a sigh)
and I bathe in the sun
of the deep blue sky.

The Waiting Room 2

The waiting room is dreary shades of blue
as I sit here unknown to any of you.
The upholstered chairs mimic Starry Night,
and nothing in here seems alright.

Apprehension and fear stifle breath.
I wonder which of one you faces death.
This floor is designed in a bloody color;
what a horrible choice; was there no other?

The blue fits the mood, the blood stokes fear.
How unpleasant it is to be waiting here!
I always thought that I would go first,
That you'd follow me, behind that hearse.

I wondered what you'd eat after I was gone.
Who'd iron for you when you're left alone.
I never thought of being here without you.
of having to fend; Lord, what will I do?

The room has emptied; I'm left here alone
with Starry Night chairs and gloomy blue tone.
Now you join me on this smeary blood floor,
to spend time left as we pass through that door.

Consolation is only in what I believe,
that we'll be together after I also leave,
but I'll not forget the horror of this room,
the cheap print of lilies, and feeling of doom.

(Written when my husband was in the hospital)

Daughter

Daughter, you've let me love you
usually at arms length,
but I feel your love embrace me
even when you can't.

So independent and proud you are
refusing to weaken or submit.
My child of your father
you are my pride, my reward
and my reason.

I've witnessed your courage in awe,
wondering its origin.
Spitting back in the face of failure
while taking two steps forward
all the pieces in hand.

You win!
One way or another,
one day or another, you win.

You have given us two precious grandchildren.
We have shared our joys,
endured our pains together.
And although I try to play the mother role,
it is often you that supplies the strength needed
and I the one leaning.

I would love you no matter what
but thank you for making it so easy.

The Matchbook

In my wallet is a matchbook cover
simple words are written there,
left in haste upon my door
to let me know how much you care.

In a drawer are cards you sent,
letters expressing pain or joy.
Theses I saved to read again;
revisit the love of my little boy.

How I wish I had taped
the music you made;
the songs you sung
and the jokes you played.

I wish I had saved
the wild flowers you picked
and dried them in a book,
then I could touch the petals
and recall your starry eyed look.

I don't have to remember sad times
or the bad times we endured.
I only want the blossoms
and the sunshine secured.

I'll remember my sensitive little boy
who didn't want to hurt a bug.
I'll remember the love we shared
and each firm and gentle hug.

My memories may have gaps
but that's okay with me.
It's my mind and my choice
and it's what I want to be.

Bug Jar

Four Years Going on Eighteen

I watch him play
with bombers and "G.I. Joes".
My heart cries in pain.
His golden hair glistens
as he plays his war games
and I want to scream!

How I love him
with his beautiful olive skin,
and blue eyes that can
put "Newman's" to shame.
A smile that can cure
a failing heart,
this boy of my blood and my name.
and I want to scream!

Don't! Don't play that deadly game!

I watch him
lying there, belly down,
his toys all around,
and imagine him fixed
on some foreign ground,
waiting…to play his game.

And I want to scream!

A Child

A ray of sunshine
in the mist
of a storm,

revealing beauty
new, pure,
and warm.

Awakening life,
stirring emotions,
giving love form,

propagating joy,
just by
being born.

Disconnected

I scream into the darkness,
no one sees my sound.
No one hears my form.
I yell my obscenities
into the nothingness!
Why do I expect a response?
Void does not possess intelligence.
The senses cannot sense
in a vacuum of oblivion.
So why do I scream!
Even with the coming of dawn
you cannot see!
You cannot hear the sunrise
on fire like me.
You see only your daily
mechanical sounds.
You hear only your goal
endless, unrewarding to your soul.
Never hearing my form,
never seeing my sound.
So why do I scream?
Would you see if I was silent?

The Lie

How are you doing? I'm asked
Quickly…I don my mask
I'm doing great! I reply
in a convincing practiced lie

I'm still able to do what I must
I continue on, to build their trust
but inside pain grips my gut
I straighten…held tight in my rut

Hard to conceal physical pain
but my lie I easily sustain
It's been hidden for a long time
but I can't hide it in this rhyme

To forgive is righteous I'm told
I say I have, but it gets old
Over and over, pain you can't see
easily hidden but not from me

Will it help to bare them here
or only hurt those I hold dear
Perhaps if I vomit them out
I'll feel better and no longer pout

Losing my mother at the age of four
Divorce, anger and lies were bore
an empty space filled by rejection
a new mother incapable of affection

I grew believing a love not there
my heart lying that she did care
Others knew, obvious to them
I was the very last, to condemn

Without my father loving steady
Becoming woman I'd not been ready
Approval and courage were his gifts
helped me stand straight, face the rifts

Rejection seemed to follow me
but I never let others really see
I lost a baby…that no one knows
Then one grown as sadness grows

I must forgive but I can't forget
as rejection and pain haunt me yet
I have given all…I'm hollow now
Proclaiming still, I am fine, I vow

Maybe if I say it often enough
I will be…but man it's tough
So many friends through it all
If you need me…please just call

Daddy raised a determined child
but the years have now defiled
my heart broken left in chards
my pain unspoken to disregard

And so…the lie continues on
I'm fine, I say, but pretense gone
I'm not…nor will I ever be
Fine…again, it's abandoned me

SHHH!

Shhh!

Moments run into hours of push,
tomorrow I'll have the time.
No, not now...this time is mine,
I'll not be guilty of neglect!

Shhh!

I know your needs my life,
Mundane as they are...they are.
I'll ignore your existence
You cannot be here now.

Shhh!

You're making me uncomfortable!
I know the windows are dirty, be silent!
I must write this poem now!
This time is mine...I don't want to cook

Shhh!

I'm Tired

I'm tired.
That empty tired.
That hollow place
that seems to suck
The "Want to" right out!
That tired that settles
in your arms and legs
like fifty pound weights
and your head's so heavy
you can't hold it up.
That tired that makes you
want to curl up in a ball
pull the covers over your head,
not because you're sleepy
but because of what you dread.
That tired…

I'm Resting

I'm
resting
in my chair,
across the room.
You smile at me there,
posed in your best attire
captured for eternity,
now framed, so I may see my family.
I glance to my right and there sits time,
Reminding me it's passing while I rhyme.

If Only On These Pages

I shall have love

if only on these pages.

I shall have tenderness

and many warm engages.

A love that will cure me

of all my empty pain.

Love so all consuming

that I'll not hurt again.

I'll feel the gentle touch

of love upon my shoulder

and the unnerving gaze

of lust growing bolder.

I'll feel love in its melting

as its fever stokes the fire.

I'll feel our bodies smelting

becoming one in our desire,

and the undulating violence

of emotions gone wild,

then lie embraced in silence

helpless as a child.

And in my wildest dreams,

if only on these pages,

I shall know love

enduring all the ages.

Memories Escape

It's late in the night.
Sleep evades me.
Memories haunt me.

The night is cold
and lonely
and I wallow in it.

I force my eyes shut
but pain persists,
escaping in all the corners.

All the corners of my mind,
burning my cheeks
on its way out.

Why

I wished I could lose my inhibitions out loud to my friend.
She said, "No you don't."
Her response lingered long after we had parted.
I battled with it as I tried to reason why.
Why would she say that?
Why wouldn't I enjoy being free?
Free of the tethers that have held me in my place for so long.
After all, everyone laughed at the poem that prompted my wish.
Why would it be so bad if I were a little wicked?
Just once, a little crude enough to be shocking!
I reached deep into the musty unused place,
the places I try to avoid, to try to find why.
It was long ago I visited this place.
It is fragile with age. It needs dusting.
Old dust, cobwebs, smells of neglect.
Why, can't I let go?
Maybe it's that four letter word.
Where is it?
Idiot! It was about sex. Yeah, sex.
Can you find that stored in here anywhere?
Ah, yes, there it is, but what's this?
Love.
Love - my four letter word - that is why.
Why didn't I remember? It's all here.
Respect, consideration, support, trust,
taken for granted, love.
Comfortable, like broke in slippers, love.
Forgotten, stored with the memoirs
in the musty attic of my mind.
Love, ah yes,
love and sex go together.
That is why.
They are precious to me.
I cannot make them common.
Not in my mind, not in my heart,
not in my world, but I laughed.
I laughed, maybe I should have cried,
Why?

Behind Closed Doors

Behind closed doors secrets lie untold

of happiness and sorrow as the lives unfold

Of dreams of tomorrow and a brighter day

of fears they borrow it may not be that way.

Behind closed doors precious memories lie

of tenderness, loneliness, sounds of a baby's cry.

Of a 'Welcome Home' laughter and a last 'Goodbye'.

Behind closed doors the heart is left …to sigh.

The Waiting Room 1

Upon my neck
a cold damp breath,
a shivering wreck,
in the face of Death.

Loved ones pacing,
wearing out the floor,
know they're facing
a battle once more.

And one-by- one,
we've watched them go
since waiting was begun
so many years ago.

The waiting room clears
as each one departs,
leaving us with tears
and our broken hearts.

But still we wait
knowing very well
it's getting quite late
to wonder about Hell.

The room is empty,
now I feel his breath.
There is no sympathy
in the face of Death.

(Written when my daughter was having a very serious surgery)

My Husband

It's so hard to watch your strength wain away,

to see you struggle with pain each day.

We've been together now; past sixty years.

We've shared much happiness and also tears.

To see you struggle to mask fear and dread,

of the war in your body and what lies ahead.

Your birthday is soon though you're not one to party;

I wish you could now and were strong and hearty.

I don't know how I will live without you,

but I hope you'll be proud of how I do.

Whatever the reason I'll never know

but I'll miss you my love, until I go.

Two Little Pillows

Two little pillows that I placed in my chair,
not knowing I placed a metaphor there.

Heart shaped pillows leaning on each other,
so different yet so perfect there together.

Purchased individually at different thrift stores,
with intentions of just adding a little to my decor.

But as I've admired them it has come to me,
they are much more than what they seem to be.

They are us...in metaphor, so different but married there.
They're to be together so they make a perfect pair.

Sad...Missing Him

Sad
Lonely
Miss my man
Just wish I could
Have him home again
His chair sits beside me
The house is deathly quiet now
God's plan is still unknown to me
His plan . . . yet decisions I must make
Am I wise or strong enough . . . without him

I pray for guidance, knowledge, and courage
And to be cognizant they are there
In this quiet void I'm waiting
For the emptiness to fill
To accept the unknown
With pretense of grace
Without my man
I feel lost
Empty
Sad.

You'll Have Lonely Times

You'll have lonely times too,
if you live long enough.
Other voices now memories,
you'll start getting rid of stuff.

No need to look back.
There's nothing to change.
And even if you could,
what would you rearrange?

It's worse in the morning.
There's no one to converse,
so I sit here remembering
and write another verse.

I still love you, you know.
though you're not here to tell.
I wish to seek advice
but I guess it's just as well.

Gray Mood

The evergreens were gray today.
A freezing fog made 'em that way.
At times a mood freezes me gray too,
leaves me cold, and turns me blue.
Painful pasts seep through my mind,
there's no leaving them behind.
Many types of storms begin,
some without, some within,
and some…that will just never end!

Young... Happy

I was
young... happy
and wet behind the ears.

It was a lazy afternoon
and I was feeling so alive.

Not a negative
thought in my mind.

He was masterful in
his love-making and
I lay there lazy
with satisfaction,
thinking how wonderful
it might be tomorrow.

Our Dad

His passing won't be on the front page
of the newspapers,
for he was not famous, notorious, or powerful.
He was just our Dad.

He was just a man who believed in his country
and served it when he was called.
No, his death won't be announced
on the airways around the world,
for he was just our Dad.

He was just a man who loved his family,
who took pride in his work,
who paid his taxes and was
never a burden to his country.
No, the six o'clock news on T.V.
won't tell the world he's gone,
for he was just our Dad.

He was just that steady force
we could always depend on,
the glue that held us together
when we might have fallen apart.
No, the world as a whole will not
change because he is gone,
for he was just our Dad.

But our world will,
because our dad helped
make our world,
and we will miss him
like we would miss gravity,
and we will know he is gone.

Tribute to my father-in-law Bufford Britton

84

Yesterday

A young family member stopped by to visit yesterday.
He stayed long enough for us to feel important to him.
He's a handsome specimen;
tall, lean and Nordic looking,
with red hair on his head and face,
a ready smile and a quick wit.

He seemed to be hungry for our reminiscing,
yearning to connect with his clan.
He leaned into the conversation;
concentrated on my husband's eager stories,
and contributed when the moment was right
to prompt more remembering.

It feels good when you are in the winter of life
for the young to bring warmth into your home.
He brought along his lovely lady friend.
quiet and petite, she just listened like me,
while generations wove a connection
to a future that we won't see.

There was a pleasant air about the room
and an eagerness in my husband's voice.
His remembrances were valued
by his young nephew, and he felt it.
It warmed my old heart to see...
the past and the future meld so beautifully.

Thank you Ben Britton

Son

Things hurt him more than most; that was the crux of a weakness.
His pain...although not physical, still turned black and blue.
Hurt eroded his confidence; he encased it in his deepest recess.
He concealed it with jokes and wisecracks to me and you.

He was intelligent; learning came easy. He embodied a loving soul.
He was my son...he played the twelve string guitar like an angel.
He was gifted...carved leather beautifully; and skied like a pro.
Things hurt him more than most; he bore hurt through every angle.

Escaping hurt was difficult; he thought it made him what he was.
So how could it be left behind; would he not be complete?
With a heavy heart he carried his burden, he had to...just because.
Had he known God made him perfect, burdens couldn't compete.

With love, mom

In Memory of Butch

I was here,
Pushing into being
Kicking and screaming.
Conceived in love
Born in pain.

I was here.
I laughed and cried
Spent time dreaming,
Played in the sun
Rejoiced in the rain.

I was here.
Suffered not seeing
The weakness demeaning
Rallied in success.
Walked straight again.

I was here.
I sought and loved
Brought happiness seeming
My wife and son left
But with my name

I was here.
My life cut short
With alcohol streaming
A man stole my future
Leaving naught but disdain.

But I was here.

Forever I Miss You!

I wish I didn't understand this loss but I do.
I wish I didn't miss the very essence of you!

I can never ever stop my perpetual tears,
Even though I've missed you so many years.

The hole in my heart will always be there.
No matter how long I've been in despair.

Mothers who understand and endure this pain
Know love doesn't end as tears fall again.

There are times I feel you by my side
But others bring emptiness I can't abide.

Mothers that have lost their precious son
Will never be the same…no
It can't be done!

I Will Not Tell You Time Will Heal

I will not tell you time will heal,
But I will hold you while you cry.
I know too well the pain you feel,
I also ask the question, "Why?

Must a child die before his time?
Before he's loved his child like mine?"
I know too well the sleepless nights,
The endless tears that at random fall.
I know the searching for reason plights,
And the emptiness that is felt by all.

No, I will not tell you time will heal
Nor smugly convey that life must go on,
For I am tempered with fire like steel
Yet I know the pain will never be gone.

So if you need just someone to share,
Someone who knows and understands.
Then remember me for I'll be there,
To hear your sorrow and hold your hands.

Dedicated to Mothers like me who cry perpetual tears.

Note: Read at ground breaking of
New Mexico National Memorial of Perpetual Tears Park

So Little Time

Tantalizing fantasies
float across my mind
as I sit gripped in reality
that there is so little time.

So little time to sit in peace
and watch the clouds above
so little time to enjoy the beauty
of the mountain valley I love.

So little time to savor
thoughts of lingering hopes and dreams
so little time to stop and embrace
the ones I love it seems.

Passing Storms

The morning is gray as I peek,
my huge Ponderosa branches sway
as if dancing to a symphony in heaven.

Momentarily I glance back.
I see sunrise has colored the gray.
It's now a neon orange,
softened by a lovely coral.
I smile …knowing God has his way.

Yes, in our lives storms will come.
They pass, perhaps damage done
but the pine tree still stands.
A symbol of strength in its sway.

May I stand deep rooted
After the storm has passed
Looking for the coral sky
Of a brand new day.

It's So Hard to Choose

What will I take with me
when I leave this place?
Won't need much for sure
to give my room grace.

Not much to decorate,
a walk in bath and a bedroom,
maybe if I'm lucky,
there'll be T.V. and chair room.

Which pictures will I take?
It's so hard to choose.
I don't want to leave them,
that's too much to loose.

I know that self-reliance
is a brief and passing trait;
and I'm hanging on desperately
but it may just be too late.

The walls of home are covered
with the years of our life;
the happy ones and sad ones
and some filled with strife.

Our memories are here.
May I take those to treasure;
or will my days be blank
and no longer filled with pleasure?

Things have no importance now.
The intangible I'll be lost without.
The comfort that surrounds me
is on loan without a doubt.

But the memories are mine,
if I can keep those intact;
I'll remember hugs and warmth
and laughter when I go back.

And if the Lord so wills,
they will live long as I.
I'll savor my memories often
Behind a smile and quiet sigh.

At Winter's End

Did I do the best I could?
I move slowly in this season of my life
Knowing winter's coming.
Wonder if I've been a good wife?
How short the seasons seemed
While our children grew
And we worked and dreamed.

But...did I do the best I could?
Now leaves fall from the trees
And crackle with each step.
Mountain tops are covered in white
Winter's promise will be kept.
And it'll soon become a long night.

So...did I do the best I could?
Will I be remembered fondly?
When the cold of winter's past?
Will things I've done bring comfort
When they must recall at last?

If not Lord, let me now begin.
Give me time to reconcile
And to make amends.
Show me what's needed.
How to put it to rest.
Please leave me here
Until I've done my best!

No doubt I could do better
So please make me aware,
Of everywhere I've failed
The mistakes I've made are there.
Let me know what I must mend!
So they will say "She assailed."
When I'm no longer cold...at winter's end.

Made in the USA
Las Vegas, NV
23 November 2023

81372312R00056